South West Coa

NATIONAL 1

C000108255

WALKS ALONG THE
SOUTH WEST COAST PATH

Ruth Luckhurst

DARTMOUTH TO PLYMOUTH

A Coastal Publishing Book

Editor Alison Moss
Design Jonathan Lewis
Publishing Manager Susan Sutterby

First published in 2011 by Coastal Publishing
The Studio
Puddletown Road
Wareham
Dorset BH20 6AE

T: 01929 554195
E: enquiries@coastalpublishing.co.uk
www.coastalpublishing.co.uk
Coastal Publishing is a Sillson Communications Ltd Company

© Coastal Publishing 2011 – all rights reserved
© Aerial Photographs Peter N. Sills
© Text Ruth Luckhurst

ISBN 978-1-907701-03-0

British Library Cataloguing-in-Publication Data
A catalogue record for this book is available from the British Library.
All rights reserved. Except for the purpose of review, no part of this book may be reproduced,
stored in a retrieval system, or transmitted, in any form or by any means, electronic,
mechanical, photocopying, recording or otherwise, without the prior
written permission of Coastal Publishing.

Any views or opinions expressed in this publication are solely those of the author and
do not necessarily represent those of the publisher.

In the interests of your personal safety and enjoyment of these coastal walks,
Coastal Publishing and the South West Coast Path Team recommend that
you follow fully the relevant safety advice in this book and the Countryside Code.
The South West Coast Path Team and Coastal Publishing can
accept no liability whatsoever.

Printed and bound in China.

Front cover image: Bolberry Down looking towards Soar Mill Cove.

With great thanks to the South West Coast Path Team's partners, who help to maintain and
manage the Coast Path, for providing pictures and contributing to the research for this book.
In particular, we'd like to thank the South Devon Area of Outstanding Natural Beauty (AONB),
the National Trust and Natural England, as well as all the wonderful photographers who have
supplied their pictures for use in this book.

South West Coast Path

NATIONAL TRAIL

Image Acknowledgements
(key: t:top, m:middle, b:bottom, l:left, r:right, c:centre)
Images in this book are copyright of the photographers and artists.

© Front cover Andy Milsom; © National Trust Photo Library/ John
Hammond 4-5, David Noton 59tr; © Andreas Byrne 5tr, 36–37; ©
South Devon AONB 8, 9tr, 29tl, 44, 45b, 58–59; © Ruth Luckhurst
9br, 14t, 14br, 15b, 22mr, 23, 45tr, 52b, 53t, 63t; © Natural
England 18t, 49tr, 48–49; © Cookworthy Museum, Kingsbridge
19tr; © Ray Culmer 19tl; © David Eales 22t; © Anne Shepherd 28t;
© Marcus McCheyne 29tr; © Andy Hay rspb-images.com 29br; ©
Philippa Chalkley 37bl; © Amanda Threlfall 48; © Fiona Barltrop
52tr; © Sarah Brigden 53br; © Eleonora Pavlovska 62–63.

Coastal Publishing and the South West Coast Path Team have made every reasonable effort to locate, contact and acknowledge copyright owners and
wish to be informed by any copyright owners who are not properly identified and acknowledged so that we may make any necessary corrections.

CONTENTS

The South Devon section of the 630-mile South West Coast Path National Trail takes in the most spectacular coastal landscapes, from tree-lined estuaries to rugged cliffs, sandy beaches and sheltered coves. This walking guide includes a selection of the best walks in the area that covers parts of the Coast Path between Dartmouth and Plymouth and offers unique glimpses into the historic relationship between people and the sea, as well as beautiful coastal wildlife and breathtaking scenery.

Whether you want an easy afternoon stroll with the family or an energetic hike over rugged cliff tops, you will find the right walk for you in this book. The walks vary in length, time and level of difficulty to suit different occasions or times of year.

They are all circular with the exception of Walk 2 between Strete and Blackpool Sands, where you have the option of catching a bus back to the start or returning by an alternative route. They take half a day or less to complete and the longest, from Plymouth, has plenty of places to stop off for refreshments en route. It's always worth making sure you allow enough time to rest at one of the many pubs and restaurants along the way, or to reward yourself at the end of the walk. The estimated timings for each route are based on a moderate pace, without taking time to stop and admire the views and so you may well take a bit longer.

Follow the route directions and look out for the recognisable acorn symbol on waymarkers and signage along the way.

Within this book there are many highlights, including Walk 5, which takes in the villages of Beesands and Hallsands, the former revealing a traditional fishing community and the latter putting the perils associated with the sea into sharp focus. In contrast, the historic ports of Dartmouth and Plymouth in Walk 1 and 18 are great bastions of our maritime heritage and demonstrate their relative success in defending the land from man and the sea.

The jagged rocks around Start Bay and Prawle Point in Walks 6 and 7 provide some challenging walks, with rewarding

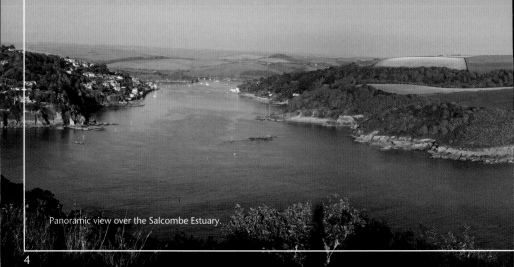

Panoramic view over the Salcombe Estuary.

4

views east and west along the coastline. The iconic Start Point lighthouse and the coastguard lookout at Prawle Point add to the features of interest along these routes. Around the Salcombe Estuary the landscape is more undulating and there are some steep sections towards Bigbury Bay. It then becomes more gentle leading up to Kingsbridge, with grassy headlands and wide open views. The final leg past Kingston (Walk 15) and into Plymouth becomes a more urban stroll along the waterfront, where the fascinating remnants of coastal defences offer a glimpse into the past of the largest city in the South-West.

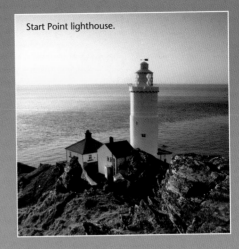
Start Point lighthouse.

Public Transport

Dartmouth and Plymouth have good transport links to bus services in the area and the main train lines to and from the county.

Most walks give information about the nearest car park. Information about public transport services for these walks can be found online at www.southwestcoastpath.com.

The Traveline South West website provides up-to-date information about all public transport links. Visit www.travelinesw.com or call 0871 200 22 33.

Warren
Point

short
cut

short
cut

Dartmouth
Castle

P

Start/Finish

Warfleet Cove

WALK 1 – Dartmouth Castle and Little Dartmouth

Distance	4 miles (6.5km)
Estimated time	1½ hours
Difficulty	● ● ● ● ●
Ascent	360ft (110m)
Map	OS Explorer Map OL20
Starting point	SX 874492

Notes: A beautiful walk rich in history and wildlife, on paths, lanes and bridleways. There are spectacular views over the River Dart, and the route visits the fifteenth-century castle and the seventeenth-century Civil War fort. The ground is sometimes uneven underfoot and there are some steep climbs.

From the National Trust Redlap car park at Little Dartmouth, pick up the South West Coast Path and head downhill towards the coast at Warren Point. Turn left here to travel eastwards with the Coast Path and follow it around the point and above Willow Cove. Ignoring the path leading inland on your left, carry on around the coast, past Compass Cove and Blackstone Point, Ladies Cove and Deadmans Cove, until you come to Castle Road. Turn right to stay on the Coast Path and follow it to Dartmouth Castle.

From the castle carry on along the river, past One Gun Point, to Warfleet Cove, where the route hits a T-junction. Turn left, and at the junction of the vehicular entrance to the old pottery there is a signposted path back up onto Gallants Bower. Follow it through the woods until it drops you back on Castle Road. Turn right and follow the lane and bridleway, past Little Dartmouth Farm and back to the car park at the start of the walk.

WALK 1

The fifteenth-century castle, owned by English Heritage, is just one of four defences built here to defend the town. Dartmouth was a significant port from the twelfth century, when the Normans realised its maritime value and used it as the assembly point for the European fleets leaving for the second and third crusades.

Above the car park area at the castle you can see the curtain wall and tower, which are all that remains of the fourteenth-century fort built by John Hawley (the man who inspired Chaucer's 'Shipman' in *The Canterbury Tales*). Hawley was a local merchant, privateer and former mayor of Dartmouth who successfully led the defence against the French in what became known as the Battle of Blackpool Sands. Immediately below the car park, to the south, is the Second World War gun shelter. To the east is the site of the nineteenth-century coastal defence battery, while above it is St Lawrence's Tower, a lookout from the time of the Napoleonic Wars.

Also within the complex is St Petrox Church, established as a monk's cell in 894, while across the river is Gommerock, built during Edward IV's reign to accommodate the chain that was strung across the water from Dartmouth to Kingswear in times of crisis.

The River Dart has been of great strategic importance since the twelfth century, and there are a number of fascinating fortifications on both sides of the river.

Gallants Bower, on the hillside above, was constructed by the Royalists between 1643 and 1645 to defend Dartmouth and its castle from attack by the Parliamentarians. A second Civil War fort was built across the river at the same time, at Mount Ridley. Gallants Bower was besieged in January 1646 and the Royalists eventually capitulated.

Gun battery at Dartmouth Castle.

Warfleet was once a separate parish from Dartmouth. Its name comes from the original Saxon 'Welflut', meaning 'Well by the Stream'.

There are several lime kilns around the cove. Until the nineteenth century limestone and coal were brought here in sailing barges and burned in layers in the kilns to produce lime, which was used as a fertiliser for the soil.

At one time there was a paper mill here, built in 1819, with the largest waterwheel west of Bristol. It made high-quality paper, on which Dartmouth banknotes were printed. It was used as a flour mill and a brewery, until after the Second World War, when it produced detergent and then pottery. In the 1950s and 60s Dartmouth Pottery employed more than 200 people, and its wares included the famous 'gurgling fish jugs'.

Dartmouth Ferries

There are three ferries across the River Dart: the Higher Ferry, the Lower Ferry and the Passenger Ferry.

The Higher Ferry, also known as the Floating Bridge, is a vehicular cable ferry which crosses the river to the north, bypassing the narrow streets of Dartmouth and Kingswear. It was authorised by an Act of Parliament in 1830 and was originally steam-powered.

South West Coast Path walkers generally cross the river on either the Lower or the Passenger Ferry. There are records of a ferry running from here as early as 1365, and in 1867, when a steam ferry supplemented the rowing boat, this was sometimes used to tow the 'horse boat', which could carry a horse and cart across the river.

Strete

Start/Finish

Blackpool
Sands

WALK 2 – Strete and Blackpool Sands

Distance	3 miles (4.75km)
Estimated time	1½ hours
Difficulty	● ● ● ● ●
Ascent	645ft (197m)
Map	OS Explorer Map OL20
Starting point	SX 841468

Notes: A short walk with stunning coastal views. There is a brief stretch of steep descent, followed immediately by an equally brief section of steep ascent, with additional gentle ups and downs, but there are good facilities for recuperation by the beach.

From the centre of Strete follow the main road (A379) north-eastwards and go over the stile to your right after about 100 yards. Follow the South West Coast Path through the fields, stopping to note the fantastic coastal views – Start Point, Torcross and Slapton Ley to the south, and the daymark tower at Froward Point to the north.

After crossing the steep Landcombe Valley, the path heads inland through fields to join an ancient green lane leading to Blackpool Sands. After about 150 yards, cross the stile into the field and follow the path to the beach.

On leaving Blackpool Sands, you can either catch the regular bus or walk an alternative route back, retracing your steps briefly to the point where the Coast Path heads left off the green lane. Continue straight ahead to join the A379 briefly before turning right onto the tiny lane. Follow it to a road into the village. Turn left to return to the start of the walk.

WALK 2

11

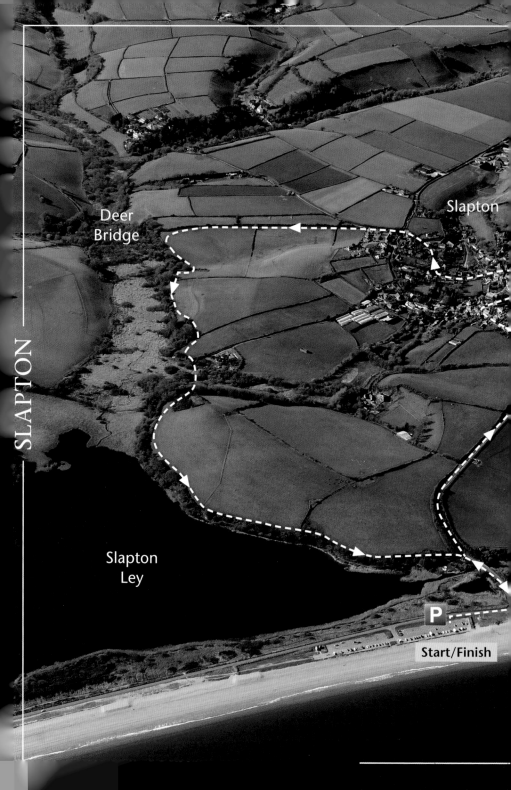

SLAPTON

Deer
Bridge

Slapton

Slapton
Ley

P

Start/Finish

WALK 3 – Slapton

Distance	3.5 miles (5.75km)
Estimated time	1½ hours
Difficulty	●●●●●
Ascent	300ft (91m)
Map	OS Explorer Map OL20
Starting point	SX 828442

Notes: A gentle stroll around peaceful countryside, starting along the shores of Slapton Ley National Nature Reserve, a beautiful freshwater lake and a Site of Special Scientific Interest for its rich variety of wildlife. Please note that dogs should be kept on a lead through the nature reserve to avoid disturbing the wildlife.

From the car park at Slapton Sands turn right along the road, then first left, signed Slapton. After about 200 yards turn left onto the public footpath signed for Deer Bridge. Follow the path along the shore of the lake. When the path leaves the waterside, just after the quarry, turn right along the footpath and follow it to the road beyond. Turn left on the road and follow it into Slapton, forking left after Wood Lane.

When the road forks again, take the footpath to the left, following it past Kimberley Nurseries to the track beyond. When the track meets a path, turn right onto this path, and when the boardwalk comes in from the left, bear right along the footpath signed to Deer Bridge. At the road turn right uphill and bear right shortly afterwards. When you come to Townsend Cross go straight over, bearing right when it forks, and follow the lane down and around to the left. At the junction at Brock St Cross turn right and, after passing the Queen's Arms, follow the road around to the left. From here follow the path along the side of the road back down to Slapton Sands.

WALK 3

Slapton Ley National Nature Reserve is recognised as one of Britain's most important wetlands.

Slapton Ley National Nature Reserve extends from Torcross (see Walk 4) to Strete Gate and is protected from the sea by a shingle bar that runs all the way along this stretch of coastline. Slapton Ley is 1.5 miles long and is made up of two parts, the Lower Ley and the Higher Ley, the former being the largest natural lake in south-west England. Although the narrow shingle bar is the only barrier between the ley and the sea, it is nonetheless entirely freshwater. Surrounding marshes, reed beds and woodland provide excellent feeding and breeding grounds for numerous species of birds, mammals, butterflies and moths.

Detailed surveys of species found here are carried out at regular intervals and highlight an enormous range of wildlife. Mammals from roe deer down to pygmy shrews live here, with otters, stoats, bats and dormice making frequent appearances.

Birds spotted in the area include hobbies, kingfishers, marsh harriers and red kites, as well as songbirds such as stonechats, song thrushes, Cetti's warblers, sedge warblers, willow warblers and reed warblers, whitethroats and blackcaps, reed buntings and cirl buntings. Adders and common lizards are sometimes to be seen, as are eels.

Elusive common lizard.

As well as mute swans and mallards, flocks of up to 1,000 of the little black coots can be seen on the open water. The Lower Ley is also home to several hundred ducks, chiefly diving ducks, during the winter months. Flocks of stocky little pochards and the larger black-and-white tufted ducks can be seen in great numbers. Small groups of the stiff-tailed ruddy ducks are sometimes to be found, and of the black-and-white goldeneye. Dabbling ducks include wigeon and teal, and occasionally a long-tailed duck or a goosander (a large diving duck with a 'sawbill' beak for catching fish) makes an appearance. Elegant great crested grebes and black-necked grebes are spotted now and then, alongside eiders and common scoters (both sea ducks), as well as great northern divers, the UK's largest diver.

Butterfly numbers have reduced in recent decades, following changes in farming practices, but numerous species abound in the reserve. Sightings include commas, gatekeepers, green-veined whites and marbled whites, meadow browns, and small and large skippers, as well as the more common tortoiseshells, peacocks and red admirals. There are many varieties of moths, too, such as elephant hawkmoths and privet hawkmoths, six-spot burnets and the striking silver Y, named after the silver marking in the shape of that letter of the alphabet on each brown wing. The careful habitat management here also encourages other insects, including the shimmering emperor dragonfly and the beautiful demoiselle.

The material which constitutes the shingle bar was pushed up by the rising sea levels during the 5,000 to 10,000 years after the last glacial period, in a similar process to the one that formed Chesil Beach, the famous shingle barrier further east, in Dorset, which also traps a lagoon behind it. Beaches formed in this way are continually reworked by coastal processes, but if a large quantity of shingle is removed from the area, the sea does not wash in enough material to replace it.

Although it is called Slapton Sands, it is shingle rather than sand that makes up the long bar that separates Slapton Ley from the sea.

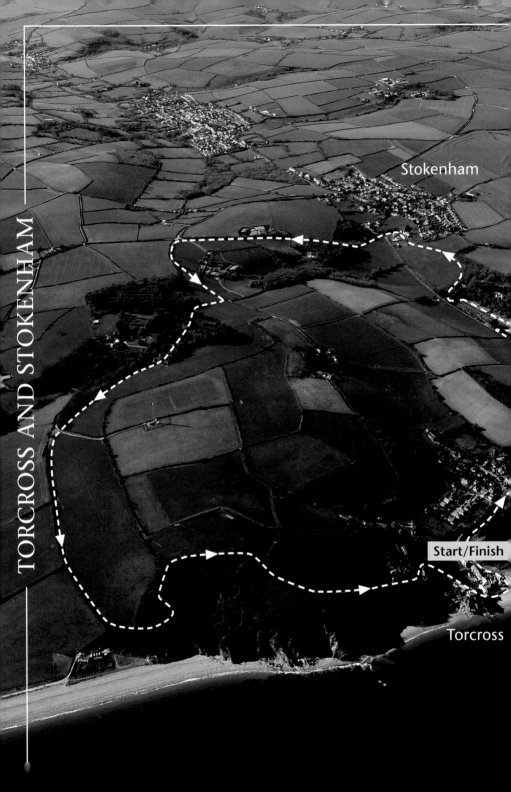

TORCROSS AND STOKENHAM

Stokenham

Start/Finish

Torcross

Slapton
Ley

P

Walk 4 – Torcross and Stokenham

Distance	4.5 miles (7km)
Estimated time	2 hours
Difficulty	● ● ● ● ●
Ascent	393ft (120m)
Map	OS Explorer Map OL20
Starting point	SX 822420

Notes: A gentle but inspiring walk through an area rich in wildlife, including the National Nature Reserve at Slapton Ley, an inland freshwater lake divided from the sea by a shingle bar (see Walk 3). Near the start of the walk there is a Sherman tank which commemorates those who died in Start Bay during Exercise Tiger in 1944. There are two short uphill stretches, but neither is steep.

Start in the centre of Torcross, outside the Start Bay Stores, with the waters of Slapton Ley on your right. With your back to the Stores, turn left and cross the road. Continue alongside the road to join the marked permissive path to Stokenham, which runs beside the road. At the Stokeley Barton Farm Shop entrance, leave the roadside by the path and follow it to the caravan site. Turn left along the drive towards the entrance, then bear right and continue straight ahead past the reception and facilities block. At the far end go straight on past the water point, cross a lane and continue on the path ahead to the field beyond, then onwards to Stokenham Church.

Pass through the churchyard to the car park and cross the main road (A379) to take the minor lane almost opposite. Follow this lane uphill for a short way, then bear right by an old barn, along a green lane which continues to climb, signed

Torcross village and Slapton Ley.

as a public byway. This levels out and then reaches a junction of surfaced lanes. Turn left and keep left at the fork. After passing the entrance to Mattiscombe Farm, there is a junction with a narrow lane on the left. Opposite this lane, on the right, is a public footpath. Go through the gate onto this path and cross the field. Walk along to the wood, keeping it to your right, and through another metal kissing gate at the top. At the surfaced drive turn left for just a few yards, then bear off right along a path into trees and shrubs.

This path emerges at a stile into a field. Walk along the left-hand boundary to another stile. Cross this and descend along the left side of the next large field to the gate in the bottom left-hand corner. Go through and bear right, then almost immediately left, keeping the farm building to your right. Continue down the track and take the right hand of two gates ahead, into a green lane. Cross the stream

and then climb with the path to meet a wide track leading into Beeson. At the first junction in the village turn left, downhill, and follow the lane round to the right. At the next junction turn left.

The road descends, turning right, then left. After the double bend, at the sharp right-hand turn by a metal gate, bear off left to a stile. Cross this, then follow the right-hand boundary down towards the sea. Carry on, crossing two more stiles and then the green ahead, to the track next to the boulders.

Turn left onto the South West Coast Path, continuing along the track and following it inland to the left, as it becomes a footpath beside the cottages. It descends as it heads back towards the sea, crossing a field and finally dropping down some steps and under a tunnel onto the end of the beach at Torcross. Turn left to return to the start of the walk.

This Sherman tank commemorates the loss of life during Exercise Tiger in 1944.

American troops in Slapton preparing for the D-Day invasion of France during the Second World War.

In December 1943 the British government evacuated around 3,000 villagers from Start Bay, so that Allied troops could rehearse the landings for the planned D-Day invasion of France. This area had been selected for its similarity to the designated Utah sector on the coast of Normandy, being a lake divided from the sea by a strip of land and then a gravel beach. Exercise Tiger here was to last from 22 to 30 April the following year.

The exercise took place in Tor Bay as well as Start Bay, and 30,000 troops on nine large Tank Landing Ships (LSTs) prepared for their mock landing, supported by the Royal Navy. Two destroyers, three motor torpedo boats and two motor gun boats patrolled the entrance to Lyme Bay, with another patrol of motor torpedo boats watching the Cherbourg area, where German E-boats were based.

On the evening of 27 April 1944 a convoy of eight LSTs was heading for Brixham, escorted by HMS *Azalea*. At the same time, a group of nine German E-boats was leaving Cherbourg on a routine reconnaissance mission in the Lyme Bay area. Stumbling across the convoy of LSTs, they opened fire. The torpedoes hit the ships before there was time to launch the lifeboats and hundreds of soldiers and sailors were trapped below decks, going down with the ships. Others leapt into the sea but drowned or died of hypothermia. In all 946 men were killed during Exercise Tiger.

For many years the scale of this disaster was kept secret. In 1984 one of the tanks that was lost just offshore was recovered and now stands in Torcross car park as a memorial to the serviceman who lost their lives.

Green Lanes

Green lanes are a distinctive feature of the South Devon AONB. These are often ancient packhorse and drovers' tracks that have left an extraordinary legacy of hidden routes running between tall hedge banks, often with overhanging trees. Some of these unique routes have been eroded, storm damaged and overgrown with time. When properly cleared and maintained, they provide a wonderful way to explore the countryside and create an outstanding haven for plants, birds and other wildlife.

WALK 4

BEESANDS AND HALLSANDS

South
Hallsands

North
Hallsands

P

viewing
platform

Start/Finish P

Beesands

WALK 5 – Beesands and Hallsands

Distance	3.75 miles (6km)
Estimated time	2 hours
Difficulty	● ● ● ○ ○
Ascent	656ft (200m)
Map	OS Explorer Map OL20
Starting point	SX 819405

Notes: A relatively easy walk with only a little up and down, travelling past the 'Village that Fell into the Sea'. The massive power of the sea is only too obvious here as the shingle rumbles on the floor of the bay with the movement of the water, especially on a windy day when the waves crash onto the rocks at Hallsands, throwing spray high into the air.

Standing on the shoreline at Beesands facing the sea, turn right along the seafront and walk to the end of the road. Bear right onto the South West Coast Path here, by the house called Seathatch. Follow the Coast Path along the cliffs and drop down to Hallsands. Walk across the beach and pick up the Coast Path on the far side as it climbs through to South Hallsands. Seaward of the new apartments a short path leads down to a viewing platform overlooking the remains of the old village, perched precariously on the rocks. Return back to the road and follow it heading inland. A little further on, opposite Trout's car park, turn right over the stile, onto the footpath. Follow the fence line through the fields and onto the green lane.

Reaching the road, turn right and go through Bickerton. At the left-hand bend, beside 'Tolcott', bear right onto the green lane signed Bridgeway Lane. Turn left at the road and then shortly afterwards, beside the stream, turn right

WALK 5

The last remnants of South Hallsands are very exposed to the elements as they huddle together on the cliff face.

onto a track and follow it onto the green lane beyond. At Higher Middlecombe Farm, bear right along the green lane, following the red waymarker. Turn right when you reach the surfaced road, then right again a little way beyond, following a green waymarker this time, pointing to Beesands. At the bottom of the field as you descend towards the sea, turn left following the waymarker. Turn left onto the Coast Path at the end and retrace your steps to Beesands.

Villagers all round Start Bay depended on fishing for their livelihood for centuries, but now it is mostly for crabs and lobsters, as this collection of creels shows.

At the end of the nineteenth century, *Fairweather's Guide to Salcombe* said of Hallsands: 'It does not seem to possess a square foot of soil in the whole place. It looks as if it properly belonged to the sea, and had only been borrowed from it for a time.' At that point the village consisted of just two rows of houses, set closely together on the 14-foot raised beach. Within a generation the sea had called in its loan.

There was a chapel at Hallsands in the sixteenth century and the village probably

started to grow around it during the seventeenth century. The noted Victorian walker-writer Walter White spent a night in the London Inn in 1854, and by 1891 there were 159 people – mostly crab fishermen and their families – living here, in 37 houses. However, around this time it was decided to expand the naval dockyard at Keyham, near Plymouth, and dredging began offshore from Hallsands to provide sand and gravel for its construction. This was proposed by marine construction engineer and Devonport MP Sir John Jackson, who was knighted for the harbours, locks and docks he built worldwide. Villagers protested, fearing the impact dredging would have on the shoreline, but it was believed that tidal action would restore the shingle to the beaches and dredging went ahead on the Skerries Bank in 1897.

Tidal action failed to replace the lost shingle, and a storm in 1903 wiped out the outer row of houses at Hallsands, and a sea wall was built to protect the settlement. This, too, was ineffective and a massive gale in 1917 undermined the remaining houses, leading villagers to abandon their homes before these too fell into the sea. They were rehoused in the cottages looking across the valley.

While the story of Hallsands falling into the sea is well known, less familiar is the plight of Undercliffe Lakes, a village that once clustered under the cliffs below Strete (see Walk 2), at Pilchard Cove. According to local historian Thomas Brice, writing in 1802: 'In the seventeenth century a considerable village existed on the north-eastern extremity of Slapton Sands, called Undercliffe Lakes, near Dartmouth. It has entirely disappeared; and within the last twenty years several

houses and above ten acres of land have been carried away by the sea.'

Little is known about the village, other than that it was relatively large and, like the other villages along Start Bay, it specialised in fishing, herring in this case. It is thought that it must also be the village once known hereabouts as both Startgate and Streetgate, situated where Strete Gate is today. A village on the shoreline is mentioned in a document from the 1740s referring to '...the cottages at Streate Sands', of which there were 17 at the time; and it seems likely that this too is the same village by a different name. By 1787 the village (by any of its names) had disappeared from local maps, so it is assumed that it was swept away some time before this, although there was mention of ruined cottages along the shoreline as late as the end of the nineteenth century.

Like Hallsands, Beesands was in existence by the sixteenth century, and was also a fishing community. By the middle of the nineteenth century there were dozens of fishing boats working off Beesands beach, hauling in catches of crab and lobster, eel and cod. A few boats still go out to supply the local inns and restaurants, but the general decline in fishing in south-west England and further storms in 1979 reduced the business to crab fishing and tourist angling.

A more tranquil vista waits the walker at North Hallsands.

Start/Finish

P

Great
Mattiscombe
Sand

Nestle
Poin

Hallsands

Start
Point

WALK 6 – Start Point and Great Mattiscombe

Distance	2 miles (3.25km)
Estimated time	1¼ hours
Difficulty	●● ● ● ●
Ascent	459ft (140m)
Map	OS Explorer Map OL20
Starting point	SX 821375

Notes: An adventurous walk over a dragon's tail of spiny rock formations, with views right across Start Bay, a visit to a lighthouse, abundant wildlife and a secluded sandy beach. The path is quite narrow and exposed in places and involves walking on rock, so it's best not to attempt it in bad weather.

From Start Point car park follow the track down to the lighthouse. The lighthouse was built in 1836 and is frequently open to the public. Retrace your steps up to the South West Coast Path fingerpost at Nestley Point and turn left.

Retrace your steps up to the Coast Path fingerpost and turn left. This next section through to Great Mattiscombe Sand can be quite rough underfoot and in places runs close to the cliff edge, so take care. The rocky outcrops make Great Mattiscombe a popular place for bouldering – low-level rock climbing carried out without ropes. Grey seals like the rocks, too, and can sometimes be seen here. In late winter and spring you may be lucky enough to see one or two white pups with them. And in the summer watch out for basking sharks just offshore. It's a great place for bird watching as well.

Above Mattiscombe Sand take the track that branches off inland, travelling uphill alongside the stream, to return to the car park.

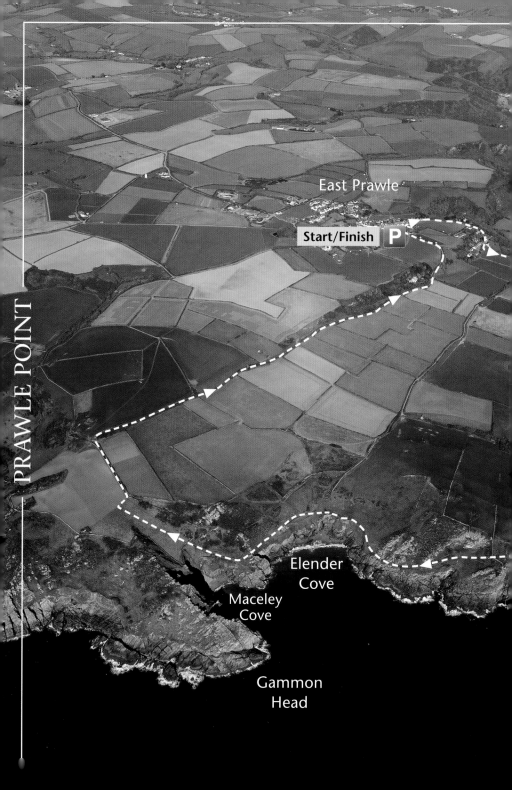

PRAWLE POINT

East Prawle

Start/Finish P

Elender Cove

Maceley Cove

Gammon Head

Langerstone
Point

Prawle
Point

WALK 7 – Prawle Point

Distance	3.75 miles (6km)
Estimated time	2 hours
Difficulty	●●●●●
Ascent	675ft (206m)
Map	OS Explorer Map OL20
Starting point	SX 782364

Notes: A strenuous walk around one of the English Channel's most noted lookout points, featuring striking geological features, Bronze Age farmers, smugglers and a wealth of wildlife. Uneven rocky footpaths and some lengthy ascents and descents make it a walk to be rewarded with a stop-off in the 500-year-old Pig's Nose Inn in East Prawle.

From East Prawle village green head for the lane leading from the south-eastern corner and follow it as it curves around and turns into a bridleway travelling south. Shortly after it does, a footpath leads away to the left, signposted to Gorah Rocks. Take this, and follow it to the bridleway 100 yards or so beyond, where you turn left. Stay on this old green lane until it hits the coast and the South West Coast Path.

Turn right here and stay with the Coast Path as it travels south-west and then west above the rocks around Prawle Point. Ignore the two paths leading inland either side of Langerstone Point, and the lane which heads uphill from the path shortly afterwards. After Prawle Point the path drops down the cliffs and around Elender Cove and then around a small headland above the tiny Maceley Cove. About 100 yards beyond this there is a footpath heading inland, away to your right.

Take this path, then turn left at the next waymarker and walk gently uphill, to where

Maceley Cove, East Prawle

another ancient green lane leads away to the right. Turn onto this track and follow it eastwards until it joins the road up from Prawle Point. Go left onto the road and carry on climbing into the village and back to the start of the walk.

The word Prawle comes from the Anglo-Saxon name 'Prawhyll', meaning 'Lookout Hill', and Prawle Point has seen much service as a lookout station and a signalling station. At the end of the eighteenth century it was an Admiralty lookout for French fleets, while a century later it was a Lloyd's signal station and then a Royal Navy shore signal station.

In the First World War the Royal Naval Air Service stationed biplanes here to patrol the English Channel for enemy ships and submarines, while in the Second World War there were radar stations at West Prawle and Western Cove.

Historically, Gara Rock was the local coastguard station for spotting smugglers; but in 1903 the coastguards took over the Prawle Point lookout building – which can be seen as you start to climb Prawle Point on this walk – their brief this time being to watch out for seafarers in trouble at sea. In 1982 it was abandoned, but in 1998 it was reopened by the National Coastguard Institution and is manned by volunteers. There are views east towards the mouth of the Salcombe Estuary and west to Start Point. Both the lighthouse and the lookout station can be visited at certain times, the latter depending on the volunteers' availability. See www.trinityhouse.co.uk for information on Start Point lighthouse.

Ancient stone wall near Prawle Point.

Summer flowers at Prawle.

The curious post in the field to the left as you drop down to the coast at the start of the walk is an old coastguard rocket post. This was designed to simulate a ship's mast in the training for the rocket apparatus, which was used for sea-to-land rescue before helicopters took over this role.

The area east of the point is noted for its wave-cut platform, formed towards the end of the last Ice Age, before the sea level dropped, leaving the flat strip of land above the current rock platform.

As far back as 4,500 years ago, Bronze Age farmers cultivated this land and the remnants of their field systems can be seen today on the western slopes of Decklers Cliff. A particularly striking set of standing stones marking the field boundaries can be seen, too, between Prawle Point and Gammon Head. Axe heads and swords have been found in the sea off Moor Sands, and it is thought that these were washed out to sea by storms and coastal erosion in the intervening millennia.

Migrating Species

Prawle Point is the most southerly point in Devon, which makes it an important place for the arrival and departure of migrating species of birds and butterflies. In the summer the green lanes are especially popular with butterflies, and many species can be seen here, including peacocks, red admirals, painted ladies and clouded yellows. Bird species include the cirl bunting (right), stonechat and whitethroat, while oystercatchers trawl along the shoreline looking for shellfish and gannets fish out in the waves. Seals and dolphins can sometimes be seen offshore, too, and occasionally even basking sharks.

The soft soil of the wave-cut platform and the shelter of the south-facing cliffs also provide the perfect conditions for warmth-loving bees and wasps, which burrow into the cliffs, and more than 100 species have been recorded, including the rare cuckoo bee and mason wasp.

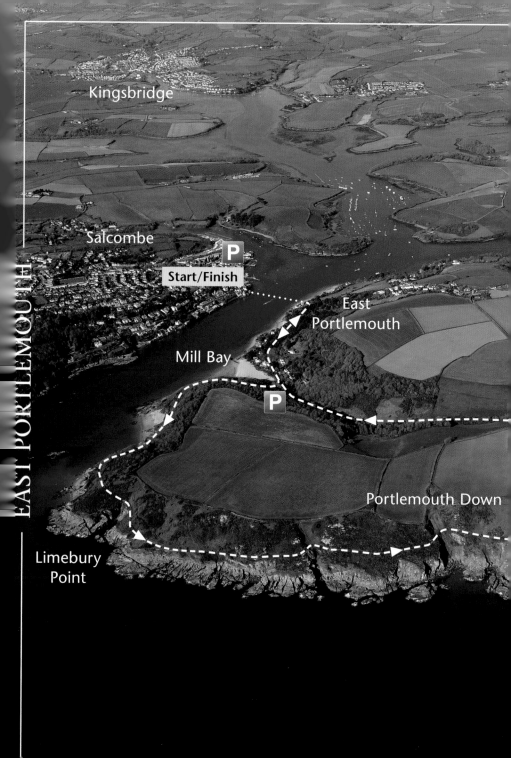

Kingsbridge

Salcombe

P

Start/Finish

East
Portlemouth

Mill Bay

P

Portlemouth Down

Limebury
Point

Gara
Rock

Walk 8 – East Portlemouth

Distance	3.75 miles (6km)
Estimated time	2 hours
Difficulty	● ● ● ○ ○
Ascent	694ft (212m)
Map	OS Explorer Map OL20
Starting point	SX 742388

Notes: A walk along the edge of the Salcombe Estuary, a waterway teeming with wildlife and the scene of a seventeenth-century artillery battle between Cavaliers and Roundheads. This walk is rocky in places, but the rest of the route is through fields and on green lanes and quiet roads, with a certain amount of ascent and descent.

From the top of the jetty steps to the ferry at East Portlemouth walk south-west along the road to Mill Bay.

On the far side of the bay, ignore the two paths to your left, leading to Gara Rock top path and the beach, and bear right, to pick up the South West Coast Path along the estuary past Hipples to Limebury Point, and over Portlemouth Down to Gara Rock. Salcombe Estuary is unusual, in that it has no river feeding it, just a number of small streams. As a result it is almost entirely a marine environment.

At Gara Rock take the path to your left that leads inland in front of the white lookout post and turn left onto the lane signed for Mill Bay. After about 200 yards pick up the footpath leading away to the left through fields to the next lane.

Bear left, back towards Mill Bay. Turn right onto the Coast Path and retrace your steps to the jetty.

WALK 8

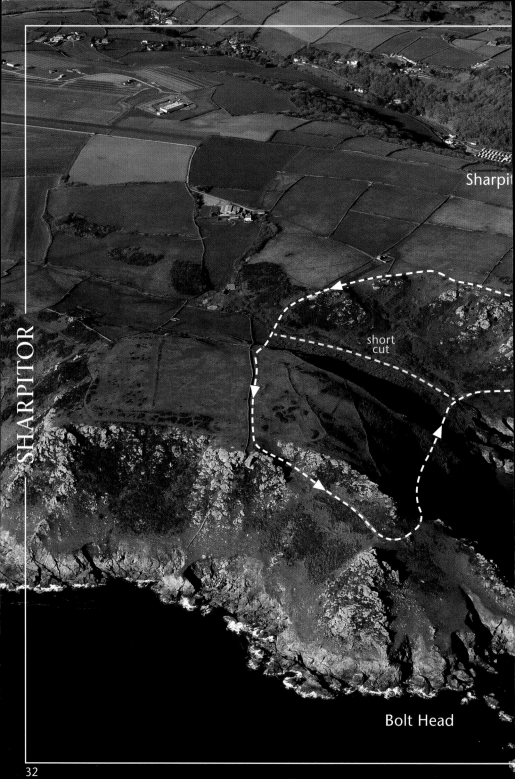

SHARPITOR

Sharpi

short
cut

Bolt Head

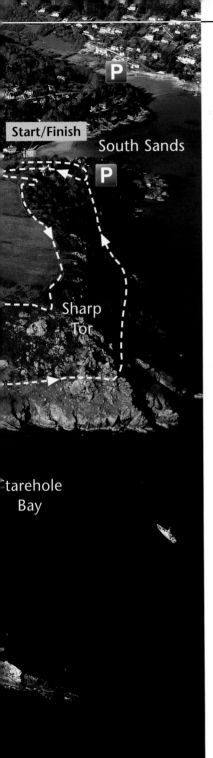

Start/Finish

South Sands

Sharp Tor

tarehole Bay

Walk 9 – Sharpitor

Distance	3.25 miles (5.25km)
Estimated time	1½ hours
Difficulty	● ● ● ● ○
Ascent	857ft (261m)
Map	OS Explorer Map OL20
Starting point	SX 728377

Notes: A walk through woods and fields, passing through a rocky landscape of impressive spires and pinnacles above Bolt Head before returning to South Sands above the Salcombe estuary. The footpath is uneven in places, with some steps and a couple of steep ascents, offering breathtaking coastal views.

From South Sands as you face the water, turn right along the road and follow it as it climbs above the beach. Carry on past the National Trust hut, along the drive that continues to climb as it winds towards Overbeck's. In front of the gates at Overbeck's turn right onto the footpath towards Tor Woods, Sharp Tor and Bolt Head.

Stay with the path as it turns left up the steps and past the compass at Sharp Tor. At the next waymarker carry on towards Starehole and Bolt Head, heading downhill. Cross the stream at the bottom of the valley and carry straight on up the steep path opposite and along the wall.

Reaching the South West Coast Path above Bolt Head, turn left and follow it around the headland. Turn left again and head back towards Sharp Tor above Starehole Bay. At the stream at Starehole Bottom, fork right with the Coast Path and stay with it as it goes round Sharp Tor on the lower path. Follow it back along the estuary, through the woods, to return to South Sands.

WALK 9

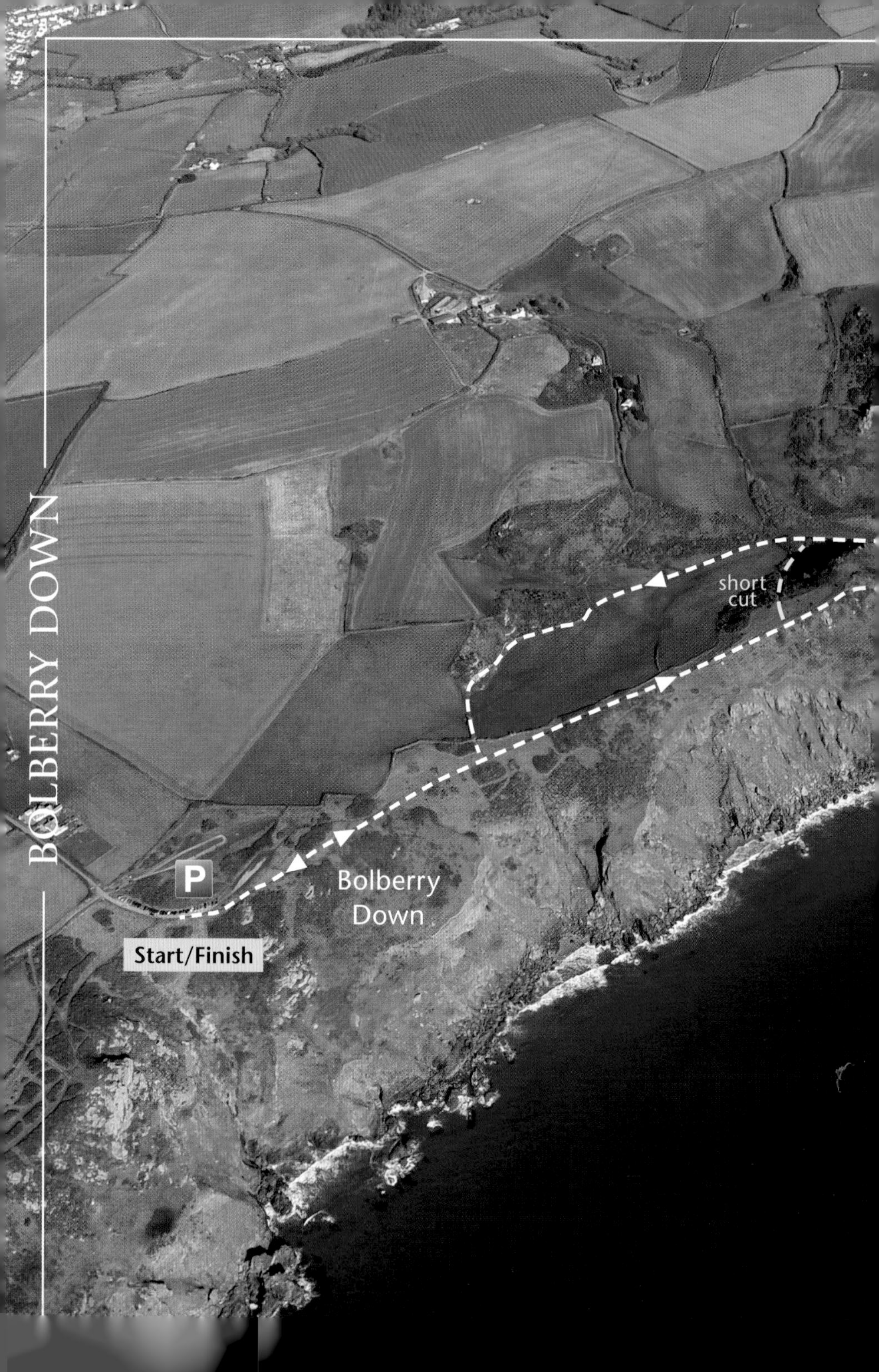

BOLBERRY DOWN

short cut

P

Bolberry Down

Start/Finish

Walk 10 – Bolberry Down

Distance	2 miles (3.25km)
Estimated time	1 hour
Difficulty	● ● ● ● ●
Ascent	406ft (124m)
Map	OS Explorer Map OL20
Starting point	SX 689384

Soar Mill Cove

Notes: A short walk on footpaths with some sharp ascents and descents and breathtaking coastal views. Soar Mill Cove can only be reached on foot via the South West Coast Path, or by sea, making the tiny sandy beach a splendid place for a picnic.

From the National Trust car park at Bolberry Down pick up the path to your left, heading south-east above the sea, and follow the South West Coast Path over the coastal heathland on West Cliff. Where the path forks, with the left-hand branch heading inland, carry on ahead along the Coast Path. When the path branches once more, continue straight ahead on the Coast Path as it drops downhill. At the bottom of the valley turn right to cross the stream and make your way to Soar Mill Cove.

Return to the path and turn left to go back the way you came, this time taking the right-hand fork after the stream. Follow the path beside another stream, climbing gently. When the path leaves the stream and another ascends steeply to the left, take this new path to rejoin the Coast Path and return to the car park the way you came. Alternatively, carry on along your path as it continues to rise slowly, curving gradually westwards. At the next fork take the left-hand path and climb more steeply up to the Coast Path at West Cliff. Turn right onto the Coast Path and follow it back to the car park.

WALK 10

Hope Cove from Bolberry Down

BOLBERRY DOWN

The National Trust manages the rare and vulnerable coastal grassland found here as a habitat for a variety of species. The area is grazed by sheep to keep the turf short and prevent scrub from taking over. Gorse is also cut back so that there is a mixture of old and young shrubs, which provide food and shelter for a wealth of wildlife, such as skylarks (listen out for them singing as they fly above), ravens (with their croaking call and acrobatic flight) and rare Dartford warblers and cirl buntings hiding in the scrub. Either side of the path there are many species of wild flowers, which in summer attract butterflies.

The schist rocks between Bolt Tail and Start Point are only found in this southernmost tip of the county and they are thought to be the oldest in Devon. Dating them precisely has been difficult because there are no fossil beds, but it is likely that they belong to the Lower Devonian period, making them over 400 million years old.

There are two types of schist here: green hornblende schist, formed originally from volcanic materials, and flaky, shiny grey mica schists which before metamorphosis was sedimentary rocks

veined with crystalline quartz.

These rocks were subjected to great earth movements after they had been laid down and the huge pressures involved have folded them into the spectacular formations to be seen around this part of the coast.

The Coast Path by the car park at Bolberry is a good place to view the grey mica schist in the outcrops around the heathland and in the cliffs which plunge to the sea.

like shales and sandstones. The two are banded together around this area, indicating that they were formed at around the same time, and they are

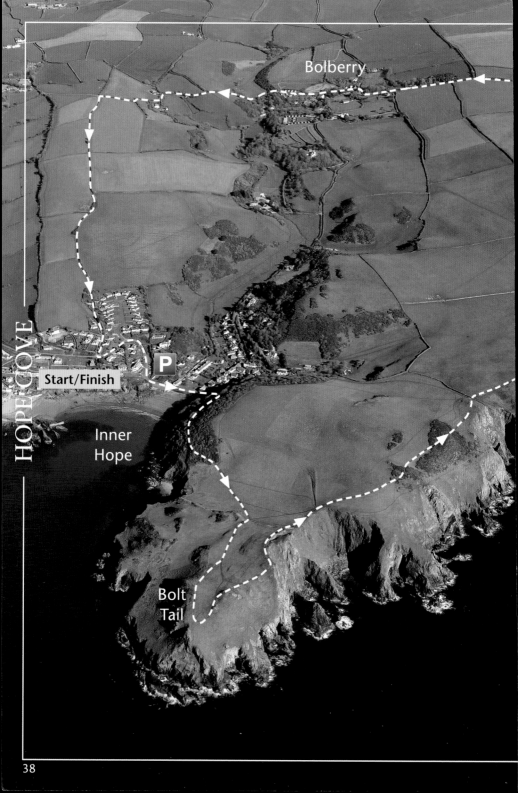

Bolberry

HOPE COVE

Start/Finish

P

Inner
Hope

Bolt
Tail

Bolberry
Down

Walk 11 – Hope Cove

Distance	4.75 miles (7.5km)
Estimated time	2¼ hours
Difficulty	● ● ● ○ ○
Ascent	719ft (219m)
Map	OS Explorer Map OL20
Starting point	SX 676402

Notes: A gentle walk along an Iron Age hill fort at Hope Cove. There's a wealth of wildlife, including skylarks and birds of prey such as kestrels, buzzards and peregrine falcons.

Turn left out of the car park at Outer Hope and follow the South West Coast Path, around Hope Cove until it reaches the slipway. Leaving the road via a flight of steps, the Coast Path heads up around Bolt Tail and onwards along the coast to the car park at Bolberry Down.

The ramparts of the Iron Age hill fort, which dates back to around 500 BC, are clearly visible as you approach Bolt Tail.

Take the road inland to Bolberry, forking left and then right through the village to carry on in a northerly direction, downhill and then up again on the far side of the stream. At the top, turn left onto Sweethearts Lane. Turn left onto the lane beyond and pick up the footpath on the right, just before Higher Barton, which leads through fields.

At the next junction of paths turn left over the stone stile and walk westwards on the footpath for about three-quarters of a mile, dropping downhill on the track beyond to the road at the bottom. Take the footpath down steps past the church and turn right onto the Coast Path to return to the car park.

WALK 11

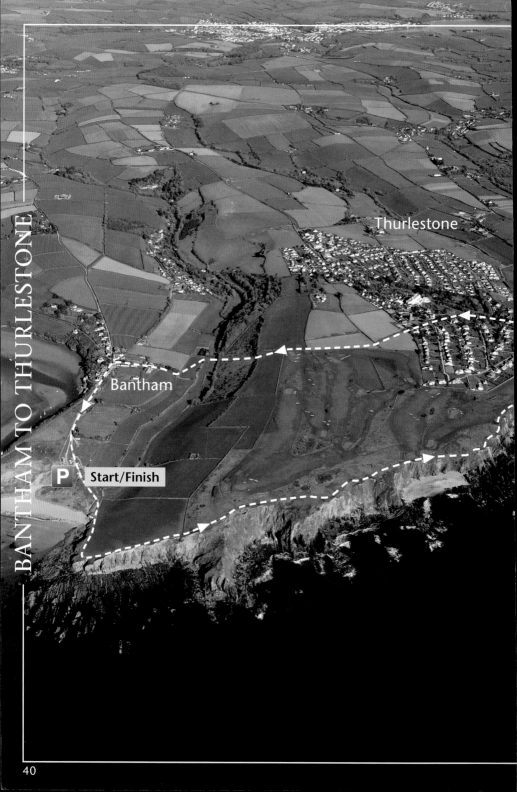

Thurlestone

Bantham

P Start/Finish

Leas Foot
Sand

Warren
Point

WALK 12 – Bantham to Thurlestone

Distance	3 miles (4.75km)
Estimated time	1¼ hours
Difficulty	• • • • •
Ascent	400ft (121m)
Map	OS Explorer Map OL20
Starting point	SX 664437

Notes: Bantham is a picturesque village of thatched cob cottages with a thirteenth-century church and a sixteenth-century smugglers' inn. On its riverside flank is Bantham Ham, the site of a Saxon settlement and, later, a Danish massacre. The walk also travels past Leas Foot Sand, a tiny sandy beach with weed-fringed wetlands.

From the car park behind Bantham Beach, fork left to go through the kissing gate and pick up the South West Coast Path. Follow it around the coast to Warren Point, ignoring the two paths heading inland.The rock arch in the bay is Thurlestone Rock, formed by wave erosion.

From Warren Point, the path heads eastwards and inland to join a lane. Follow it past the golf course clubhouse to the road. Turn left again and walk through Thurlestone to the war memorial, where you leave the road to continue along the track.

Crossing the stone stile beyond the church, follow the footpath through fields to drop steeply downhill towards Bantham, forking left just before the stream to reach the village. At the Sloop Inn turn left onto the road and follow it back down to the car park.

WALK 12

Ringmore

Ayrmer Cove

Challaborough

Bigbury-on-Sea

P

Start/Finish

Burgh Island

Bantham

Walk 13 – Ringmore and Challaborough

Distance	4 miles (6.5km)
Estimated time	2 hours
Difficulty	● ● ● ○ ○
Ascent	1,000ft (304m)
Map	OS Explorer Map OL20
Starting point	SX 651442

Notes: A walk that mixes cliff tops, sandy beaches and exploring the streets and lanes of the historic village of Ringmore, with its thirteenth-century church and inn. The route is along footpaths, tracks and quiet roads and there are plenty of steepish ascents and descents.

Starting from the main beach car park in Bigbury-on-Sea, make your way past the café and join the South West Coast Path beside the road heading north-west. When the road pulls away uphill to the right, carry on along the Coast Path, following a track that leads down to Challaborough Beach.

On the far side of the beach continue along the Coast Path as it climbs steadily up to Toby's Point. On this section, please avoid the temptation to go right to the cliff edge, as in places it is unstable and if the cliff collapses underneath you, it is a long way to fall!

Along here you get great views back to Burgh Island and on a clear day you may be able to spot the 161-foot (49-metres) high Eddystone lighthouse, built on a small but treacherous rock 13 miles south-west of Plymouth. The current lighthouse is the fourth to be built on the rocks. The first was washed away by the great storm of 1703. A replacement timber lighthouse burned

WALK 13

down, as did the third, 'Smeaton's Tower' was dismantled and rebuilt on Plymouth Hoe (see Walk 18) after the rock it was built on started to crumble.

From Toby's Point descend to the picturesque Ayrmer Cove, a beautiful sandy beach that is rarely busy even in the height of summer. After crossing the footbridge at the back of the beach, follow the track heading inland for about half a mile, past Lower Manor Farm.

When the track turns abruptly right and another footpath joins from the left, carry on along the track to the right and into the village of Ringmore. Bear left when it forks, then turn left at the T-junction to the church.

Turn right at the church and walk about 200 yards to the edge of the village, bearing left onto the track beyond. Stay with it as it narrows to a footpath, passing through fields and straight ahead to the road beyond. Cross the road and pick up

the footpath into the field opposite. This path takes you through fields to the main Bigbury road by Mount Folly Farm. Here you rejoin the Coast Path, turning right to follow it down to a seasonal car park. Near the bottom of the hill, continue following the Coast Path as it crosses the road onto Clematon Hill (owned by the National Trust) and head back to the beach car park and the start of the walk.

Ringmore is a quaint and peaceful village, with a thirteenth-century church, All Hallows, and an inn, the Journey's End, from the same century, built to accommodate those constructing the church. Many of the cottages are thatched, some of them dating back to the seventeenth century, while the manor of Ringmore is listed in the Domesday Book where it appeared as Reimore. A large part of the village is designated a Conservation Area and much of the surrounding land is owned by the National Trust.

Burgh Island.

It is thought that some of the stonework of the north transept of the church is Saxon and pre-dates the rest of the building, so there was probably a settlement here before the Normans arrived.

Sharpland rocks.

The Journey's End Inn, originally the New Inn, was named after R. C. Sherriff wrote his play *Journey's End*, depicting life in the trenches in the First World War there in 1928. It would seem that the pub had a hidden face: while it was the meeting place of the parish council, and was described in a nineteenth-century document as a 'house of good order', there was also a false wall concealing a smugglers' storeroom.

Bigbury Bay has been highlighted as an area of geological importance, because of the way the earth's movements have compressed the rocks and thrust the layers into dramatic formations. The slates and shales of the Meadfoot Beds and the Dartmouth Beds from the Devonian period meet here, and as you walk around beyond Sharpland Point you can see the folds and faults in the rocks beside you. The pink rocks are the Meadfoot Beds; their colour is a staining from the younger red sandstone rocks of the Permian period, which are found in the area.

Challaborough Beach

At one time Challaborough was Ringmore's port, and like the rest of the seafaring communities along the South West Coast Path it has a rich history involving fishing, trading, wrecks and rescues. It was from here that the fishing boats sailed for pilchards, and it was from here, too, that the rescue efforts were launched when a ship went aground, as often happened, on the vicious rocks around Burgh Island. The coastguard cottages still standing on the shoreline are testimony to the watch that was kept over maritime travellers. Coal was landed here, too, for the locals' use.

Nowadays the beach is still popular as a result of those powerful waves: surfers love it, as do divers, with all those wrecks to explore on the seabed.

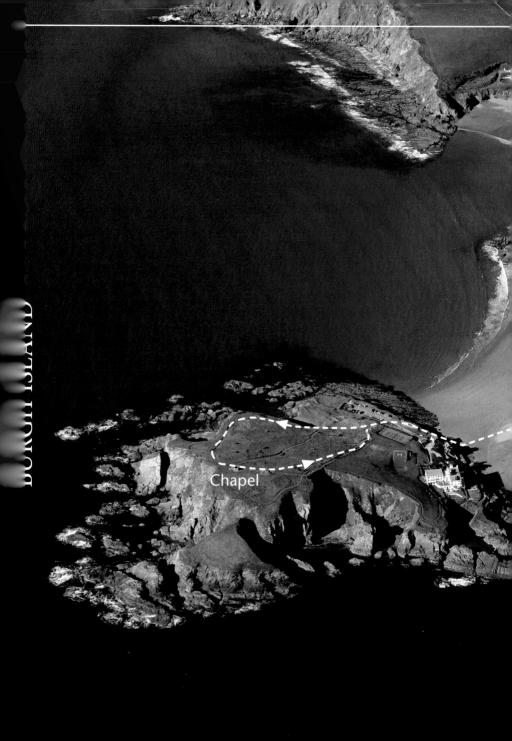

Chapel

Start/Finish

P

Walk 14 – Burgh Island

Distance	1 mile (1.75km)
Estimated time	1 hour
Difficulty	● ● ● ● ●
Ascent	132ft (40m)
Map	OS Explorer Map OL20
Starting point	SX 651442

Notes: Cross the causeway to Burgh Island on foot or go there by sea tractor (check out the times of the tides and the tractor before you leave) and see the famous Art Deco hotel (not open to non-residents), the fourteenth-century inn and the ancient chapel/huer's hut, as well as a couple of sandy beaches, all on the one very small island.

From the Marine Drive car park take the footpath to the right which goes down to the beach below, and either walk across to the island or, if the tide is too high, take the sea tractor.

On arrival, follow the footpath which goes around the island to the right, beyond the Pilchard Inn. When the path forks, the right-hand path leads down to the beach; for this walk, take the left-hand footpath, bearing right a moment later to continue around the back of the island.

At the end of the island you can explore the beach and the chapel, then take the path that carries on around the edge of the island. When it forks bear right, staying above the coast, around the point and back to the hotel, from where you can return to the mainland.

WALK 14

The island is first recorded as St Michael's Island, which later changed to Borough Island, and then to its current name. A 1765 map shows it as 'Borough or Bur Isle'. It is 275 yards (250 metres) from the mainland and is often referred to as 'part-time island' because at low tide it is linked to the shore by a sand causeway. Two pillboxes were built on the island on either side of the causeway during the Second World War due to fears of a German invasion. One of them has been converted into unique living accommodation and sold at auction.

In 1411 there was a chapel on the island dedicated to St Michael (hence the island's original name), and there was a monastic community here for some time before that. It is thought that the remains of the monastery lie under the present hotel and that the Pilchard Inn was built as guest lodgings for it.

Following the dissolution of the monastery, the island's population depended on pilchard fishing and the chapel on its summit was converted to a huer's hut. Here someone would keep a lookout for the arrival of shoals of pilchards offshore, raising a 'hue and cry' when they were first spotted to alert the waiting fishermen.

Not long after the monks left, the notorious Elizabethan smuggler Tom Crocker moved in. There was once a tunnel – it is now bricked up – connecting the Pilchard Inn to a cave on the island's western shore. This enabled him to shift his contraband out of sight of the excisemen, but they caught up with him eventually and he was shot dead in the porch of the inn.

The first hotel on Burgh Island was a prefabricated wooden hut built by music-hall star George H. Chirgwin in the 1890s for weekend parties.

In 1927 the island was sold to Archibald Nettlefold, who was a film-maker and heir to the Guest, Keen and Nettlefolds engineering company. He set about erecting the 'white liner' hotel which fronts the island today. Built in the contemporary Art Deco style, which took its inspiration from geometric shapes and combined ornamental elements from a wide range of sources, Burgh Island Hotel is now a Grade II listed building.

Walkers on Bantham Beach.

The hotel's flamboyant design attracted many high-profile visitors, including - it is said - Edward and Mrs Simpson. Noel Coward stayed here, while crime writer Agatha Christie's connection went even further, as the hotel provided the setting for two of her books, *And Then There Were None*, and *Evil Under the Sun* (the TV adaptation of the latter was actually filmed here).

The sea tractor to Burgh Island.

Churchill and Eisenhower also reputedly met here before the D-Day landings, in which South Devon played a prominent part. During the war itself, the hotel was used as a recovery centre for wounded RAF servicemen, and the top two floors were damaged by enemy bombing. After an interim period, when it was converted into self-catering apartments, it was sold again and lovingly restored to its former glory in the 1990s.

The first sea tractor, designed to carry passengers across to the high-society hotspot, was built in 1930. The third and current model uses a Fordson tractor engine and hydraulic motors and was built in 1969 at a cost of £9,000. It was designed, in exchange for a case of champagne, by Robert Jackson, a pioneer of the nuclear power programme in the 1950s.

The water in the mouth of the Avon Estuary here is unique, combining the twice-daily tidal flushing with the flow of fresh water from Dartmoor. The conditions are perfect for oysters, which feed on the naturally occurring phytoplankton and organic debris. As many as 300,000 are grown here, taking between two and four years to reach maturity. They are graded into different-sized mesh bags throughout their lifespan before being hand-picked, cleaned and sold to restaurants all over the UK.

WALK 14

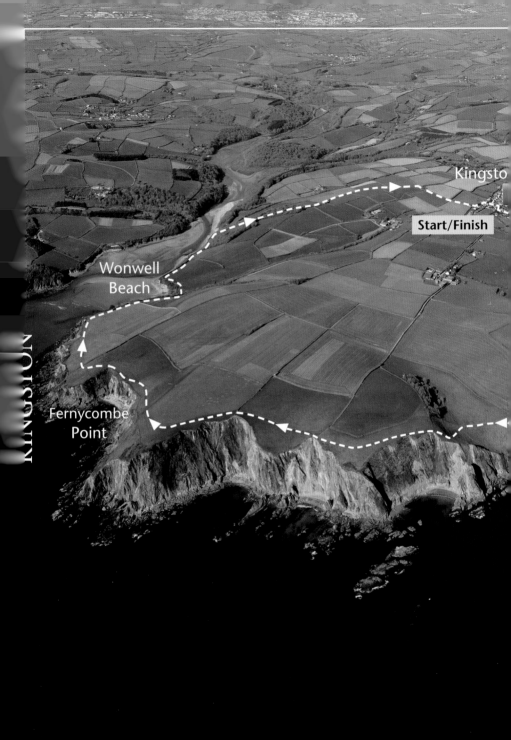

Kingsto

Start/Finish

Wonwell
Beach

Fernycombe
Point

KINGSTON

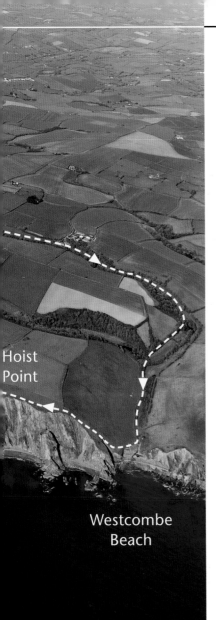

Hoist
Point

Westcombe
Beach

Walk 15 – Kingston

Distance	5.5 miles (8.9km)
Estimated time	2¾ hours
Difficulty	•••••
Ascent	954ft (291m)
Map	OS Explorer Map OL20
Starting point	SX 635478

Notes: A strenuous walk high above the sea with breathtaking coastal views. There are steps and stiles, with some steep ascents and descents as well, and the path can be muddy in wet weather. Watch out for ravens performing aerobatics and peregrine falcons diving at speeds of up to 200 miles an hour!

From the church in Kingston go past the Dolphin pub and turn right, then left. Follow the lane, staying with it as it becomes a bridleway along the track, carrying straight ahead on the footpath signed to Westcombe Beach. At the beach turn right onto the South West Coast Path and climb steeply with it to Hoist Point, following it up and down above the dramatic cliffs, ignoring the path travelling inland to the right at Fernycombe Point, until you come to the mouth of the River Erme.

If the tide is out, follow the foreshore around from Wonwell Beach to the old slipway and take this up to the road. Otherwise, carry on along the Coast Path to the steps and go down them to the lane below. From the end of the lane, carry on up the road for about 75 yards, then turn right onto the footpath into the woods. When you emerge from the woods about half a mile beyond, follow the path along the top edge of the field and through the next three fields to the road. Turn right on the road and left at the crossroads beyond to return to the start of the walk.

WALK 15

Farming has long been important at Scobbiscombe. One of the traditional fertilisers used along the coast was seaweed and here it was hauled up the cliffs to the fields above, hence the name Hoist Point.

The sheer height of the cliffs on this part of the Coast Path made them brilliant look out points in the past. Beacon Hill, along the route and 307 feet (93 metres) above sea level, was one of many places used all the way around the south-west coastline to warn of the approach of the Spanish ships of the Armada during hostilities in the sixteenth century. There would have been other beacons lit here over the centuries: celebratory bonfires for the coronations and jubilees of assorted monarchs and the anniversaries of major events like VE Day.

The coastline here has been subjected to continual erosion as storms at sea sent waves crashing into the cliffs over millions of years. As a result the shore is lined with jagged rocks and stacks and tiny islands

Erme Mouth.

– a sailor's nightmare. The most lethal of these are Mary's Rocks, hidden beneath the water at all but the lowest of tides, right at the mouth of the tranquil-looking Erme Estuary. No fewer than fourteen wrecks lie on the seabed here.

The oldest of these, and one of Britain's oldest shipwrecks, is a Bronze Age vessel, used in the local tin trade. Forty-two ingots of tin have been found on the wreck, almost

Looking back towards Westcombe Beach. Tales of smugglers and wreckers abound among this rocky coastline.

Cliffs at Hoist Point.

certainly mined on nearby Dartmoor. The vessel may have been en route to nearby Burgh Island, a prehistoric tin trading centre of international importance at the time.

The cliffs, too, have been dramatically sculpted by the action of the waves, which have created many caves along the shore. These facilitated another lively local trade, a more recent one: smuggling. On the beach at Westcombe there are caves equipped with mooring irons, while in the cliff face at Freshwater Valley there is a cave with a chimney once used as a lookout and hideaway. There are also rumours of a tunnel linking Westcombe Beach and Ayrmer Cove, and another running from Westcombe to Scobbiscombe Farm.

Some of these caves are accessible at low tide, but take care not to be cut off by the incoming tide.

Walkers crossing the sand at Erme Mouth.

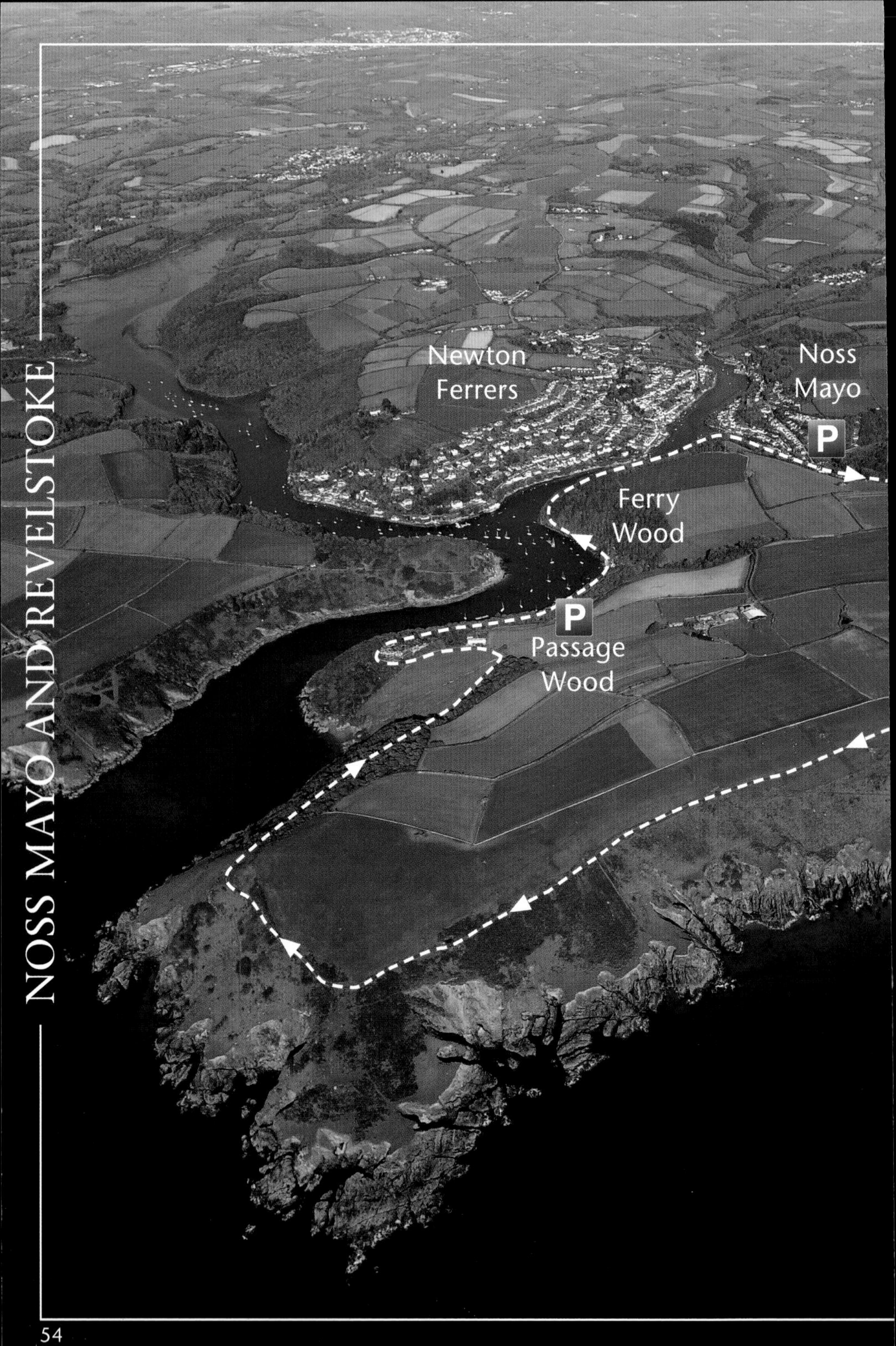

Newton
Ferrers

Noss
Mayo

P

Ferry
Wood

P

Passage
Wood

Start/Finish

WALK 16 – Noss Mayo and Revelstoke

Distance	4.5 miles (7km)
Estimated time	2¼ hours
Difficulty	● ● ○ ○ ○
Ascent	647ft (197m)
Map	OS Explorer Map OL20
Starting point	SX 541466

Notes: A gentle stroll on a historic carriageway, along an open estuary and wooded riverbanks, as well as around the wild coastline, taking in picturesque Noss Mayo with its many delightful features. The one stile is easily bypassed.

From the National Trust's Warren car park go through the wooden gate at the far end and take the track towards the sea. Follow it through a gate as it turns right to join the South West Coast Path. You are now on part of the 9-mile Revelstoke carriage drive, which was built by Lord Revelstoke in the nineteenth century to impress visiting friends. The walk follows the carriageway all the way into the mouth of the Yealm Estuary. At Passage Wood take the left-hand fork (signed Coast Path) through the woods for a more interesting route or continue along the carriageway.

At the edge of Ferry Wood (there is a small parking area) take the path that runs just above the lane, leading most of the way into Noss Mayo. At the end of this, follow the lane into Noss Mayo and through the village, turning right at the sharp left-hand bend uphill. Carry on past the car park and the tennis courts, and follow the lane as it turns into a track and heads gently up the hill, back to the Warren car park.

Heybrook
Bay

Wembury
Point

Wembury

Start/Finish

Wembury Beach

Walk 17 – Wembury Point

Distance	3 miles (5km)
Estimated time	1½ hours
Difficulty	•• • • •
Ascent	324ft (99m)
Map	OS Explorer Map OL20
Starting point	SX 541465

Notes: A fairly easy walk, with some steep but short climbs above Wembury Point's wave-cut rock platforms, where the sea teems with unusual marine life, past the Great Mew Stone, once a source of inspiration to the nineteenth-century artist J.M.W. Turner and now a bird sanctuary. Dogs should be kept on a lead, as Dartmoor ponies graze here.

From Wembury Beach car park pick up the South West Coast Path as it descends to cross the bridge behind the beach and follow it as it continues westwards along the low cliffs. After a little less than a mile you will come to a narrow path, signposted for Spring Road. Turn right up here, then fork left to climb through the scrub and at the top turn left to follow Marine Drive. This is the old access road to HMS *Cambridge* (see page 58). Turn left onto it, carrying straight on after the gate (or take the path on the left to the foreshore for a short cut back to the start).

When the path approaches the houses, turn sharp left onto the Coast Path and follow this south and then eastwards, past an old boundary stone. Reaching Wembury Point, take a short detour to the beach, with its nineteenth-century boathouse, before continuing along the Coast Path to retrace your steps to Wembury.

WALK 17

For almost a century the headland was in military use, becoming the site of the Royal Navy's chief gunnery training school, HMS *Cambridge*, in 1956. Following the closure of the gunnery school in 2001, Wembury Point was bought by the National Trust with the help of over 30,000 individual donations. The Trust has since demolished the ugly military buildings and security fences, giving uninterrupted views across to the wedge-shaped Mew Stone (or Gull Rock, as it is also known).

In the nineteenth century, warrener Sam Wakeham and his wife, Ann, lived in a little round house on the tiny island, advertising a ferry service to 'the Moonstone' for anyone on the mainland who 'holds up their white pockethanchecuffs for a signal'. Seemingly the income raised through doing this, as well as looking after the rabbits, was too meagre, because Sam supplemented it with a little smuggling.

Wembury Point is a Site of Special Scientific Interest for both its geological features and the wildlife which they support. The rocky reefs are the perfect habitat for all kinds of rockpool creatures, providing shelter for marine life even at

low tide. The species found here include anemones, shore crabs, pipe fish, sea scorpions, spiny star fish, spider crabs, Cornish sucker fish, lobsters, edible crabs and limpets. The rare and declining allis shad, a type of herring, is found in the sea here, as well as dogfish, pollock and bull husk.

The foreshore, cliffs and fields behind are frequented by numerous wintering and nesting birds, including the threatened cirl bunting, and it is a popular bird-watching spot, as there is a good chance of seeing something unusual.

The best way to discover more about the wildlife and geology of the area is to visit the Wembury Marine Centre at the beach car park, or go on one of their regular guided walks and rock pool rambles – see www.wemburymarinecentre.org for details.

The National Trust Omega sign for Wembury Point and Great Mew Stone.

WALK 17

View from Wembury Point.

PLYMOUTH SOUND

Staddiscomb

Hooe Lake

Turnchapel

P

Start/Finish

Jennycliff

Mount Batten Point

Fort
Bovisand

WALK 18 – Plymouth Sound

Distance	6.5 miles (10.25km)
Estimated time	3 hours
Difficulty	● ● ● ● ○
Ascent	678ft (207m)
Map	OS Explorer Map 108
Starting point	SX 493523

Notes: From as long ago as the Bronze Age, Plymouth has been important for seafarers. This walk visits some of the fortifications built around the Sound over the centuries for the purpose of defending it. There is one long, steady climb, as well as some flights of steps and a few stiles, but there are a number of short cuts built into the route, as well as opportunities to take a bus or a ferry back to base.

From the car park at Jennycliff cross to the grassy area by the café. Take the South West Coast Path along the low cliff in the direction of Plymouth, heading towards a large white stone. Pass this, and another, then carry on to the path in the bottom corner of the field, signposted Breakwater. Keep to the path signed to the Breakwater, climbing the hill to Mount Batten and then going down the steps. Continue on the waterside path, which leads to the ferry from Plymouth Barbican. (The route could be started from here if arriving by ferry.)

Pass the ferry and continue on the waterside path. Follow the marked Coast Path for Turnchapel through the Yacht Haven area. At the top of the steps go left and left again, into Turnchapel. Turn right at the end just before the MOD gates. Follow the lane and at the end turn right, then left along the head of Hooe Lake, after this bearing left uphill through Hooe. You can get a bus from here back to Jennycliff or into Plymouth.

WALK 18

Reaching the top of the hill follow the left path then fork almost immediately right. At the junction at the end, go left downhill, then turn right alongside Radford Lake. When the path emerges into open parkland, leave the surfaced path and bear right onto another path which skirts the lake. Stay on the path ahead to arrive at a main road. Cross this and take the path on the opposite side, signposted Erme-Plym Trail.

At the grassy area bear left. Follow the path past some houses then into woodland, forking right in the woods. Keep climbing through the woodland, bearing generally to the right. After a stile, take the uphill path opposite, turning left at the top, along the field-side track – still signposted Erme-Plym Trail. Continue through three fields, bear right to cross a stone stile, along another field, and then down some steps to arrive at Staddiscombe. (Turn left and follow the lane for the village shop and buses to Plymouth.)

At the foot of the steps turn right, then bear almost immediately left along the minor lane. At the bottom go straight ahead next to a gate onto a stony track. After reaching the drive at the bottom bear slightly left along the path below and keep generally parallel to the road. This leads to the Coast Path at Bovisand. Turn right up the steps and continue ahead past the small car park, seasonal café and bus stop.

From Bovisand, follow the Coast Path back to Jennycliff. Bear right at the cottages then turn right up a flight of narrow steps before the second terrace of cottages. At the top the path crosses a bridge, then another flight of steps leads to the walls of the old rifle range. Keep to the Coast Path, bearing left through the wooden gate when the path approaches the road. At the time of writing, the final section of Coast Path leading back to the start of the walk at Jennycliff has had to be closed due to a landslip and walkers are diverted onto the road above. Take care here as the road has no footway. It is hoped that the cliff can be stabilised and the Coast Path reopened.

From Jennycliff there is a superb view over Plymouth Sound. From left to right it encompasses the Breakwater, Penlee Point, Kingsand and Cawsand, Mount Edgcumbe, Drakes Island, the Tamar Estuary and Plymouth, with the Hoe foremost.

Plymouth Hoe and the Citadel.

Radford Lake.

Mount Batten is a defensive site dating back to the Bronze Age. More recently it became a seaplane base, with squadrons of RAF flying boats. It ceased to be used by the RAF in 1992. The defensive tower on the summit dates to the 1650s and the Dutch wars. There are views from here over the Sound, Sutton Harbour (Plymouth's original port) and the Cattewater, which is the estuary of the River Plym. Mount Batten Breakwater stretches out into Plymouth Sound, giving splendid views, especially of the Citadel opposite. Yet another defensive work, the Citadel dates to the 1660s.

Fort Bovisand, just off route, was one of the ring of forts built to defend Plymouth by Lord Palmerston in the nineteenth century. Never used in war, they became known as Palmerston Follies. Fort Bovisand is now a diving centre.

Hooe Lake is a tidal creek off the Plym Estuary. 'Lake' in this context reflects an Old English word for a watercourse. Note the piers over the water, which carried the old railway branch from Plymouth to Turnchapel.

As well as the South West Coast Path, two other long-distance paths meet here at the side of the lake. The West Devon Way runs to Tavistock or Okehampton, while the Erme-Plym Trail leads to Ivybridge and the southern end of another trail, the Two Moors Way.

Radford Castle and Causeway were built in the mid-nineteenth century. Despite the castle's appearance, it is not a defensive site but was built as accommodation for the estate's 'keeper'. The estate was the home of the Harris family, local landowners and friends in their time of Sir Walter Raleigh, and the open parkland above the lake was formerly part of the estate, as was the arboretum beyond.

WALK 18

Covering 630 miles from Minehead to Poole, the South West Coast Path National Trail leads you through diverse landscapes, all with their own unique story to tell. If the walks in this book have inspired you to find out more about the longest and most popular of the UK's 15 national trails, visit the website at www.southwestcoastpath.com.

Natural England
Natural England is the government's adviser on the natural environment and provides the majority of the funding for the maintenance of the Coast Path, which is undertaken on a day-to-day basis by Devon County Council and the National Trust. Through Environmental Stewardship schemes, Natural England also helps farmers and other landowners to protect and enhance the countryside so that nature can thrive. Visit www.naturalengland.org.uk.

South Devon Area of Outstanding Natural Beauty
The South Devon AONB is a protected landscape of national importance and covers 337 square kilometres (130 square miles) of coastline, estuaries and countryside. To explore the South Devon AONB visit the website, which has over 50 downloadable walks and trails, with maps, directions and commentaries: www.southdevonaonb.org.uk.

National Trust
The National Trust Countryside Team works seven days a week to restore and care for the characteristic wildlife of the area, as well as working with local communities to improve access and understanding of these special areas. Regular events and opportunities to get involved mean that all ages can help shape their countryside. Visit www.nationaltrust.org.uk.

South West Coast Path Association
If you enjoyed these walks, why not join the South West Coast Path Association? This charity represents the users of the trail, campaigns to improve the path and raises money to help it happen. By joining you'll be one of thousands who help to make the South West Coast Path one of the world's greatest walks. You can find out more, and buy a range of Coast Path souvenirs from their website, www.southwestcoastpath.org.uk.

Staying safe on the Coast Path
As well as following the Countryside Code, when you are on the South West Coast Path remember:

- Staying safe is your own responsibility – please look after yourself and other members of your group.

- Keep to the path and stay away from cliff edges – please follow advisory signs and waymarks.

- Take special care of children and dogs – please look after them at all times.

- Dress sensibly for the terrain and weather – wear suitable clothing and footwear and be ready for possible changes in the weather.

- Stay within your fitness level – some sections of the Coast Path can be strenuous and/or remote.

- In an emergency dial 999 or 112 and ask for the coastguard.